Damselflies

by Colleen Sexton

D1482642

BLASTOFF!
2
READERS

Note to Librarians, Teachers, and Parents:

Blastoff! Readers are carefully developed by literacy experts and combine standards-based content with developmentally appropriate text.

Level 1 provides the most support through repetition of high-frequency words, light text, predictable sentence patterns, and strong visual support.

Level 2 offers early readers a bit more challenge through varied simple sentences, increased text load, and less repetition of high-frequency words.

Level 3 advances early-fluent readers toward fluency through increased text and concept load, less reliance on visuals, longer sentences, and more literary language.

Level 4 builds reading stamina by providing more text per page, increased use of punctuation, greater variation in sentence patterns, and increasingly challenging vocabulary.

Level 5 encourages children to move from "learning to read" to "reading to learn" by providing even more text, varied writing styles, and less familiar topics.

Whichever book is right for your reader, Blastoff! Readers are the perfect books to build confidence and encourage a love of reading that will last a lifetime!

This edition first published in 2009 by Bellwether Media.

Library of Congress Cataloging-in-Publication Data
Sexton, Colleen A., 1967-
  Damselflies / by Colleen Sexton.
    p. cm. — (Blastoff! readers. World of insects)
  Includes bibliographical references and index.
  Summary: "Simple text and full color photographs introduce beginning readers to damselflies. Developed by literacy experts for students in kindergarten through third grade"—Provided by publisher.
    ISBN-13: 978-1-60014-190-4 (hardcover : alk. paper)
    ISBN-10: 1-60014-190-0 (hardcover : alk. paper)
  1. Damselflies—Juvenile literature. I. Title.

QL520.S49 2008
595.7'33—dc22   2008019871

Contents

Damselflies are long **insects**.

Most damselflies live near ponds, streams, and **wetlands**. These places have shallow water.

Damselflies begin life underwater. They **hatch** from eggs.

Young damselflies are
called **nymphs**.

Nymphs grow slowly and **shed** their skin many times.

Soon, nymphs crawl out of the water. They shed their skin one last time.

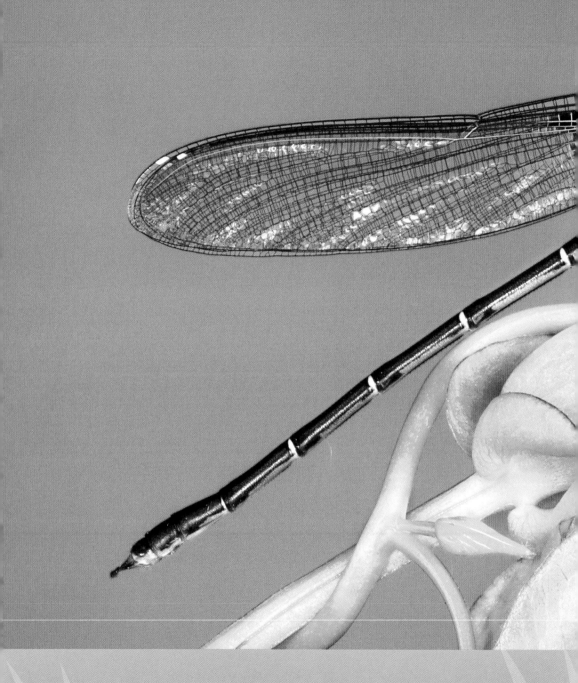

Nymphs become adults.

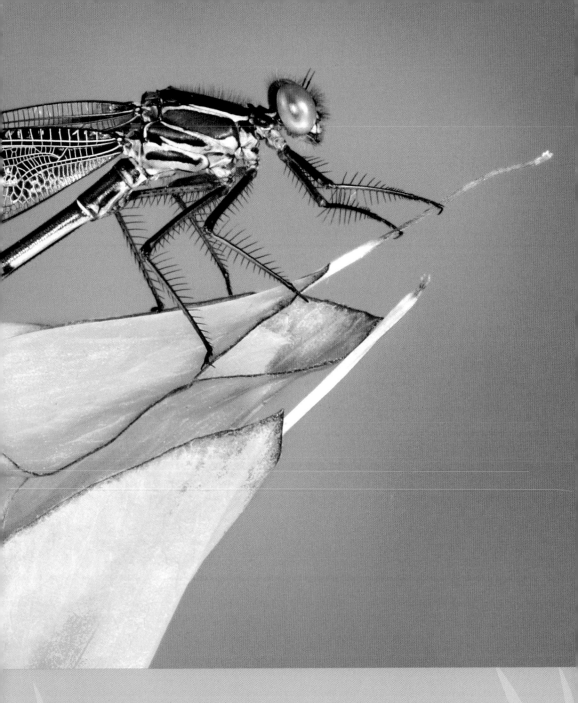

Damselflies have thin bodies.
They can be blue, red, yellow,
and other bright colors.

Damselflies have four wings shaped like paddles.

Veins make a pattern on the wings. The veins make the wings strong.

Damselflies spread their wings to fly. They can fly backward, sideways, and **hover** in the air.

Damselflies fold their wings together when they rest.

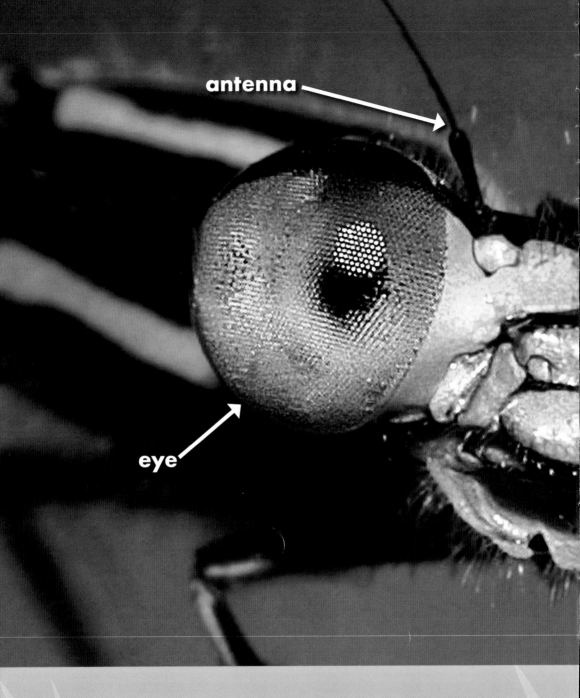

antenna

eye

Damselflies have big eyes
that are set far apart.
Damselflies can see very well.

16

antenna

eye

Damselflies have short **antennas**. They use their antennas to feel and smell.

jaws

Damselflies have jaws
with teeth.

Damselflies have six long, hairy legs.

Damselflies fold their legs together like a basket when they hunt.

They use their legs to grab insects. Damselflies will eat any kind of insect they can catch!

Glossary

antennas—the feelers on an insect's head; insects use their antennas to touch and smell things.

hatch—to break out of an egg

hover—to stay in one place in the air

insect—a small animal with six legs and a body divided into three parts; there are more insects in the world than any other kind of animal.

nymph—a young insect; nymphs must grow and shed their skin many times before they become adults.

shallow—not deep

shed—to let something fall or drop off

veins—hard tubes in an insect's wings; veins make the wings strong and able to bend.

wetlands—land where the ground is wet and soggy most of the year

To Learn More

AT THE LIBRARY

Kuhn, Dwight. *Dragonflies and Damselflies*. Detroit, Mich.: Blackbirch Press, 2005.

Nikula, Blair and Jackie Sones. *Stokes Beginner's Guide to Dragonflies*. Boston, Mass.: Little, Brown and Company, 2002.

O'Neill, Amanda. *Insects and Bugs*. New York: Kingfisher, 2002.

ON THE WEB

Learning more about damselflies is as easy as 1, 2, 3.

1. Go to www.factsurfer.com

2. Enter "damselflies" into search box.

3. Click the "Surf" button and you will see a list of related web sites.

With factsurfer.com, finding more information is just a click away.

Index

The images in this book are reproduced through the courtesy of: Cathy Keifer, front cover, pp. 10-11, 15; Tim Zurowski / age fotostock, pp. 4-5; Rene Krekels / Foto Natura / Getty Images, pp. 6-7; Valentin Rodriguez / age fotostock, pp. 8-9; Papilio / Alamy, p. 12; Cisca Castelijns / Foto Natura / Getty Images, p. 13; Michael Durham / Getty Images, p. 14; blickwinkel / Alamy, pp. 16-17, 21; Jef Meul / Foto Natura / Getty Images, p. 18; Mark Heywood / Alamy, p. 19; Arco Images GmbH / Alamy, p. 20.

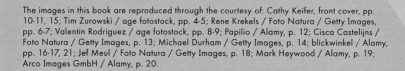